Swimming

Carousel Readers

Annette Zuidland

Illustrated by Steve Pileggi

DOMINIE PRESS

Pearson Learning Group

ISBN 1-56270-722-1

Printed in Singapore
3 4 5 6 7 8   07 06 05

Dominie
Press
Pearson Learning Group

1-800-321-3106
www.pearsonlearning.com

The turtle jumped
into the water
and swam away.

The duck jumped
into the water
and swam away.

The seal jumped
into the water
and swam away.

The fish jumped
into the water
and swam away.

The otter jumped
into the water
and swam away.

The dog jumped
into the water
and swam away.

The kangaroo jumped
into the water.

And he stayed to play
all day.